Fried Chicken, Schmussy & Other Songs From a Baptist Hymnal

Fried Chicken, Schmussy
& Other Songs
From a Baptist Hymnal

poems by

Alicia Young

LEAKY BOOT PRESS

Fried Chicken, Schmussy & Other Songs From a Baptist Hymnal
by Alicia Young

First published in 2015 by
Leaky Boot Press
http://www.leakyboot.com

Copyright © 2015 Alicia Young
All rights reserved

No part of this book may be reproduced or transmitted in any form or by any means, electronic, mechanical, photocopying, recording, or otherwise, without prior written permission of the author.

ISBN: 978-1-909849-24-2

For Manny Feuerberg, a prince of Tennessee, and the biggest schmussy magnet who ever swaggered through darkened, whiskey lit barrooms and fine dining establishments this splendid world has to offer…see, I keep my bets, friend.

And Bob.

And Seb.

And Mom.

…my sons

Jesus…

…and the first shepherd who noticed

the goats went crazy after eating certain beans…

Contents

he was	9
The Endurance	10
judgment and peppermints	11
the better bomb	12
the dogs are unfed	14
spinster sisters	16
breakfast with hemingway	19
i will burn your fucking bonsai trees	20
apocalypse noir	21
crocuses	22
i saw them slow dancing	23
stomped grapes	24
ashes & tangerine peels	25
France	26
my uncle martin the 7-foot giant	27
drink the ocean	28
turn of the century	31
smoke rise	32
tying the knot	33
malala	34
burn	35
cause enough for perfume	36
sweet nothings	38
ancestry	39
every wayward penis	40
Anne Boleyn	41
a little shop of kinks	42
winter was a crime scene	45
war makes murderers	46

flash paper	47
future farmers of america	50
home from the war	53
Have you ever stopped to think?	55
softened fruit	56
all told in an altoid tin	58
lover's leap	60
southern gothic	61
the autism primer: year 18	63
suicide tourism	65
soho diner	67
street magician	68
our neighbors would hate us	69
sepia toned lithograph	71
cement truck philosophy	72
posthumous letter	74
aruba	76
this day and for the rest of time	78
50 year plan	80

he was

i loved him so much
he was
the crack in my voice
before i cried

The Endurance

our love
was a wooden ship
of grand design
built atop the tallest building
in our city skyline
knowing well
it would never
touch the ocean

judgment and peppermints

Winter has been left
at the altar
by Spring
in a Kentucky church
full of faded wood panels
battered hymnals
pews creaking with
suspicious Baptists aghast
carrying tissues
judgment and peppermints
in pocketbooks
bathed in beams
of stained glass light
containing confederate
dust particles descending
certain of
gossiping daffodils
and death

the better bomb

i blame
the self esteem movement
of the 1970's
for our loss of humility
me-monster generations
of inflated egos
with honorable mention ribbons
butterfly blinking their vapid eyes
this is america
we're more concerned
with the packaging
than the contents
of our
food
entertainment
government
character
conscience
watch a super bowl half time show
to learn
why other countries hate us
but what more
can we expect
from a country founded
on the impossible
a world to colonize
an ocean away
puritans turned pentecostals

politicians
who invented
the better bomb
committing genocide
legislating slavery
as they handle snakes
solicit our vote
and speak in tongues

the dogs are unfed

depression has a heart
buried beneath
pumice streets
of old Pompeii

it has lost
all interest
in homeric greek

walled within
the house of the tragic poet
it doesn't pretend
to engage in platitudes

it does not want to tell you
how it's doing

it does not want
to be reminded
of how much it aches

how embarrassed it feels
or infect you
with its tragedy

it has forgotten its father's birthday
depression can't elaborate
regarding dreams as
a fool's currency

lacking the wherewithal to say

i feel as though
i died years ago

the horses are dead
the dogs are unfed
the natives have ceased
their drum beat

spinster sisters

when i was a little girl
allowed to roam
through the backrooms of
the house shared by my great aunts
ancient
spinster sisters
jo ann and mary alys
whose Bates brothers all passed before
i didn't mind the obligatory visits
imposed by my mother and sister so much

finding photographs of glory faded
antique wash basins and ceramic kittens
delicate baubles in satin boxes
fine dresses who had given up on finding love
bobby pins on china saucers atop
a vanity avoided because no one wanted to see
what it had to show

until i was five i thought jo ann
was a man
an old farmer in mens clothes
who smoked constantly
cut her hair short
and squatted like our indian ancestors
talking of her land
loyals dogs
sturdy tractors
whose barn had burned

tidbits you orta know
a lesbian of a time one didn't acknowledge
such things
baptist blasphemy running through
her country bones

mary alys
the once beautiful bride
whose wealthy husband cecil had died
leaving her childless
grieving
though she seemed content
to remain married to his ghost
so feminine she was
pin curls
perfectly filed long
nicotine yellow nails
too many rings
a forked tongued
wicked gossip
oral histories
slim pointy nose
judging everyone whilst wearing
pink polyester and
knee high panty hose

two women were never more different
yet to me
they were symbiotic halves
of a singular tale of family woe

jo ann on her side of the sitting room
reading the paper
and mary alys
applying ponds cold cream to her face
and lotion to her transparent
blue veined soft hands
claiming she intended to make
a pretty corpse

jo ann went first
ate up with cancer
mary alys died later
of meaness
i suppose

breakfast with hemingway

i shared a meal
in a bombed out madrid hotel
with ernest this morning

he was grimy and blackened
from a night
of wandering through the plaza de la villa
amidst the sheep, soldiers, and ghosts

i ordered red wine and white cheese
he barked for whiskey and bread
all of which continuously slid to our right
down the half broken bar
to the east

under the swaying
provisional wartime bulbs

my pristine cream blouse
looked like sacrilege
stretching across my breasts
and his eyes

forcing my lips to move
i asked him what he would change
about his life

he said

"I would have fucked more.
I would have written less."

i will burn your fucking bonsai trees

he could not hide
his twisted psychology
behind his volunteering
his social networking
his name dropping
his poorly translated
banal Japanese poetry
his social work
and his damned bonsai trees
that he was a control freak
with a volatile temper
and a duplicitous nature
that he is the man in the bar rubbing his
chino covered cock on your thigh
condescending
manipulative
overly solicitous and hell bent
on getting his penis
into your vagina
anyone's vagina
perceiving female poets
as emotionally compromised
easy targets
and if his unfortunate victim muse
was able to see his monstrous nature
through his kabuki mask
she was condemned by him publicly
as a crazy woman
of course

apocalypse noir

never fall in love
with a frenchman
who looks like
a handsome lumberjack

but always listen
to his opinions
about literature

paris is burning
haiti is dead
new orleans is under water

my marie laveau paper dolls
are casting voo doo spells
upon the living

and
i have so much to read
before the world ends

crocuses

now comes
the inevitable onslaught
of springtime poems
as the poets
realize
they are in fact
not dying

i saw them slow dancing

five year old
tippy toed sneaking
down the dark hall
toward the lit music
coming from the kitchen

my parents happy
i saw them slow dancing
to conway twitty
singin' hello darlin'

it was far from perfect
but it was enough
to know
what love is

stomped grapes

we knew
we would ruin each other
like wine
willing itself
into vinegar

ashes & tangerine peels

being with him
felt like
the bottom of a trash can
that had never been cleaned

France

Perhaps…
it is a failing
of my English
blood,
but some men
have an enticing way
of looking
like a war
worth losing

my uncle martin the 7-foot giant

        rounded up 8 men
        still bitter
        about being forced away from his
        english degree at the college of
        William and Mary
        and hung them from a gallows
        above fishin' creek
        for being northern sympathizers
        kicking a tree the size of god
        from beneath their feet
        as their wives and children watched
        in horror lashed to a tree
        and let me say
        to the union
        my bones are still sorry

drink the ocean

the one thing i know
how to build with my hands
i learned in eighth grade industrial arts

if you give me raw wood
a table saw with a router
a miter saw
a bit of wood glue
a plane sander
clear varnish
i will build for you
a beautiful little beveled edge box
with brass hinges
and a hasp lock

but this day
i intend to construct one
for myself
designed for securely containing
three things

this poem
the straw that broke the camel's back
and my suicide

you see
my soul died this morning
i gave up

but i am a mother with autistic

18 year old twin sons
who loves them enough
to allow her heart to continue to beat

i love them enough to remain alive
i know to do this
because my father didn't

i love them enough to keep blood
in these arms that hold them
when they are screaming and crying
and blaming me for giving them autism
by virtue of my having been the one
who gave birth

telling them
son
if we can
just survive the hormonal high school years
everything will be alright

one of them hides his asperger's from everyone
at school in a futile attempt to fit in
but he's only hiding the words
the label of autism
his actions let people know he's not typical
so when he stares too long
or has a face void of expression
they just think he's a creepy jerk
so he keeps getting in trouble
because he won't say
"i have asperger's don't take it the wrong way,
i don't mean any harm"
because he says
"i would rather be called
an asshole
than a retard"

the other one
is resistant to everything

but eating and sleeping
rules are what you break
when mom isn't looking
he thinks
so long as he says the right words
to her face
no matter if it breaks her heart
because there is no synapse that fires
between his behavior
and the consequences thereof

this morning i realized
i am attempting to drink the ocean
pissing into the wind
nothing i do
will ever be enough

but i do not have the option of giving up
i have to keep banging my head into these walls
until i am bloody
as this is my lot

this little wooden box i shall build
emblematic
of my pledge to go on with my life
to continue to fight

these words contained within it
are my coping mechanism

because in my zombie heart
i know
it is better
than my entire body
being placed into
into a finely crafted
pine box

turn of the century

how i long for
a gentler time
when courtesy was still common
people opened doors for one another
and grace was more fashionable
than a no talent reality television hooker
with an oily horse ass

when i could get on a plane
bound for miami
with a dime bag of weed shoved
up my pussy
and a pearl handled .45
in my carry-on bag

and no one seemed to mind

smoke rise

i am the seventh great granddaughter
of pocahontas
7th daughter of a 7th daughter
the smoke rise witch queen naturally reborn
as the vengeance
of a thundering Kentucky prairie
filled with the blood
of 16 thousand dead cherokees
i have come for what was taken from my people
i have come to dethrone unjust kings

tying the knot

only marry
the one
you wish to
destroy
slowly

malala

no longer reference
David and Goliath
when speaking of courage
or insurmountable odds overcome
tell me of the day
malala
book and pen clenched
in her tiny girl hand
told the Taliban
to fuck off

burn

you were
the cigarette
i didn't have
a match for

cause enough for perfume

perhaps my very existence
invites your lips

however you are the reason
i've taken to writing invisible love poems
in the finest of rust belt drinking establishments

my fingertips tracing desires
through saturday night flooded bar top wastelands
of dissipating beer foam and 7 and 7's gone errant

i've become convinced jesus won't return
to fly us all back to glory land on his private salvation jet
unless i have a bottle of wild turkey in my left hand
and your hand in my right
stumbling through 3 a.m. street lamp heavens
beside a monument to our first kiss

i've watched the english patient twice for chrissakes
my nights have become ee cummings sketches

your absence is cause enough for perfume

we could be a kate chopin novel

i want to share with you everything of value i know
i want to give you all my favorite books
i want to be the woman who pulls you into her
when you've stepped too close to the edge of the subway platform
i'll teach you which one the salad fork is without anyone
      taking a hint

i'll tell you the dirtiest jokes i know in crowded elevators
i'll buy us an old plymouth just so
i can lean over from my best girl shotgun seat
and unlock the driver's door for you
before we head to the drive-in

i want to learn to knit
just so i can knit you an ugly afghan
to cover you up with on the couch
when my fried chicken and a novel
have conspired to take you
into blissful sleep adrift

give you passed out kisses you'll never know about
and present you with the perfect hangover cure
coffee made and aspirin come christmas morning

i want to be the woman who loves you so well
she remembers
to grab the reading glasses you always forget
before we walk out the door
of this daydream
in which
i am perfectly content

sweet nothings

we were madly in love
just long enough
for your voice
to haunt me
for the rest of
my life

ancestry

sometimes
i look at photographs
of my
grapes of wrath worthy
destitute
sunday best ragged
depression sepia
tobacco creased
great-grandparents
and think
i can't believe these people
fucked each other

every wayward penis*

if she is fortunate
there comes a point
in the life of an evolving woman
when she learns to say
no
to herself and others

she recognizes the destructive patterns
and destructive people
she has repeated

she then begins to implement
a healthier method
of living

it is the moment she finds validation
inside her own skin

it is the moment
she ceases
to be dick dumb

* full title 'every wayward penis you allow inside your vagina lowers your intelligence quotient 3 points'

Anne Boleyn

479 years
after her death
women still may learn
from this fallen
queen
that loving
a tyrannical selfish prick
results
in the loss of your only head
but he will go on living
destroying hearts
ruining the world
believing himself
the rightful king
of other lands
above god
existing
happily wearing bejeweled lies
with his boils
needing lanced

a little shop of kinks

when i was 15
i had my belly button pierced

my cool ass mom
took me and my best friend renee
to permanent productions
a tattoo and piercing shop
owned by
the da vinci of body modification
in cincinnati

down on hamilton avenue

northside

the little rainbow flag bedecked
neighborhood

where my brother
would die of aids
three years later

my mom signed for me to get the piercing
she watched with delight
as mike pinched with triangular forceps
then shoved the needle through my skin

but my mom is where i get my wild

this was long before the aerosmith video
with alicia silverstone getting pierced
in a grunge plaid shirt

with her long white girl hair
that spawned a million
middle class girls to emulate her

i found this little boutique downtown
on race street
after i started to drive
called

a little shop of kinks

it was a gay clothing
sexual fetish
and art deco antique store
with the best selection
of body jewelry in town

sometimes renee and i
would take mom with us
when we went shopping there

we would peruse
the sex toy
side of the store

cages
enemas
cuffs
clamps
ball gags
a trapeze
sex swings
leather daddy
and bondage apparel
paddles
whips
and the biggest selection
of dildos you've ever seen

one day
my mom held up

a giant natural skin dong
approximately three feet long
and ten inches in diameter
at eye level

and queried loudly
in her southern kentucky accent

"Well, what in the hell do you need a root that big for?"

we died laughing
and i had never loved her more

winter was a crime scene

winter
was a crime scene
blood splattered onto frosted windows
red lipstick curse on the vanity mirror
high rise
victim dismembered
meat rotting
in poorly wrapped packages
to be toe tagged
orphans whisked away by the government
appointed neglectful
pearls fallen across the sticky floor
to a police radio symphony
Mahler fatalistic
smug detectives
sipping black coffee
no sugar to be found in the city
a glib act
notebook scratches
with no hope for answers
or finding the perpetrator
who caused
the whole mess

war makes murderers

there are but three
unchangeable forces
known
in our meager lives

history is indestructible
dying
and the passage of time

that having been said
no wrongful death
may be avenged
with the death of another

if history has taught us
nothing else
it is that
war
makes murderers
of all humankind

flash paper

when i was younger
and of a mind
to patronize
dance clubs
meat markets
irish pubs
and strobe lit
techno bars

before smoking
was banned on earth

i had a wicked little trick
for getting rid of unwanted admirers
hell bent on
not taking no
for an answer

never a smoker myself

but my best girl friend and wing man
was permanently attached
to a marlboro red

i would take little trips
to the magic store
haines house of cards

a norwood treasure

buying myself a few books
of flash paper

when extreme measures
were called for
i would casually ask her for a drag
off her cigarette
keep dreadfully calm
inhaling the death with my right hand

in my left hand
i would palm
a tiny wadded up piece
of apollo's paper

after the third
get lost, man
we already asked you nicely twice
was ignored

and his hot slurred-breath hostility
began to show

my hands would rise
as i lunged at him

with a swiftness
his jagermeister brain
couldn't process

bringing the tobacco's fire
to touch the incendiary device
at the tip of his nose

i became a witch
throwing flames
into his burning eyes
my gutteral madwoman screaming
"motherfucker
I will eat your heart while you're still alive!
RUN RUN RUN!"

you'd be surprised
how fast a bald headed

goatee and cargo short wearing
cincinnati bratwurst man
can run drunk in flip flops

the first time i pulled that slight of hand
outside the warehouse on vine
in over-the-rhine

i looked down

to find my best friend
had pissed her fishnets
laughing

there are many ways women learn
to remain alive

future farmers of america

the year i moved south
amidst a northern drought
there was a band of arsonists terrorizing
the people of three counties
comprising my childhood stomping grounds
Lincoln, Casey, & Pulaski
Kentucky

the bastards burned the hardware store
a few occupied houses
the lumber yard
and my dead daddy's high school
in eubank
where he was in
future farmers of america
a basketball star
and the first of his mining man clan
to graduate

i had moved into my grandmother's old house with my sons
to write my book
the utilities were reasonable
the memories were free

poppies and black irises in the back yard
mockingbirds in the trees
hummingbirds attending gossip socials
and a coat of many colors rose bush
who presented the sunlight back
to god in heaven each morning

one dark august night
deep into the soup thick summer heat
i had retrieved a jar of green beans
from the cellar out back
and proceeded to
cook them up with bacon grease
at the same old avocado green
electric whirlpool stove
where i watched
in hungry awe
as memaw did it
a thousand times

my loyal staffordshire bull terrier
was laying behind me at my feet
as is tradition when mama is cooking

my proximity to danger
was right beside
the side door
in the kitchen
leading out onto a breezeway
and porch

i had the big wooden door open
with only the screen door locked
in place to
allow for escaping heat
stirring
stirring
stirring
slow and southern
lost in a dying love poem

at the same moment i saw
a bit of night beyond the doorway
move in the shape of a man
up to no good
just when
i heard a gutteral growl come from

the canine creature behind me
comparable to the ear piercing howls
of a minotaur
trapped inside a labyrinthine hell

my boy
my dog Vinnie took flight
at the door
his paws never touching the floor
he exploded through the screen after
the menacing figure

i gave chase with my shotgun
saw he had three fuckers on the run
silhouette kerosene cans in idle hands
determined to burn down
what the banks
haven't reclaimed yet
their lives stripped
of purpose and pride
one generationally entrenched
welfare check at a time

that night a church went
up in smoke instead

that was the evening
Vinnie saved my life
the lives of my twin boys
and the most sacred hiding places
my childhood provided

god have pity on the lost
future farmers of america

home from the war

i went out with my friends
all dolled up
in my high class call girl best
the night after we broke up

he was tall blonde beautiful and stupid
5 years younger than me

a marine

home from the war

on leave
the groom of his wedding party

we got bleedin' drunk on 5th street
and stumbled back to the millennium hotel
buying condoms along the way

it was the place
you and i
had first met
and said goodbye
that sickening july

perfectly evil indeed
america's favorite white meat

and i fucked him
i fucked him so hard

to spite you
to eat the world

to reclaim me

to kill anything of us
still holy

Have you ever stopped to think?

Perhaps God
is a temperamental visual artist,
who is perpetually
dissatisfied with his earthly work,
so he just keeps adding more
bloody paint,
shards of garbage,
and odd designs
to trash the damned thing?

softened fruit

once you've been a mortician
you never stop thinking
or dreaming
like one

beyond exposure
to the harshest chemicals
in existence
it is the psychological blitzkrieg
that is the true
occupational hazard

i am plagued by dreams
of having to embalm
my dead since i was 6 father
his features i set perfectly
but his hands won't take the fluid
they are a sick yellowish color
with blackened fingernails
the fingers spread apart
ghoulishly
implying
death is always
grasping coldly toward us

as for the rest of humanity
my eyes see them
as softened fruit
about to spoil

each day
has become a discipline
in attempting
not to think
this way

as i find life
in all its pain and glory
to be worthwhile
and of
unfathomable beauty

all told in an altoid tin

it is in my heart to begin
to make miniature dioramas
a history of man
all told in an Altoid tin
creation
the discovery of fire
Eve tempted by the serpent
with a pomegranate
the day religion was invented
by deluded men
the battle of Agincourt
the day we discovered the new world
already had a civilization
occupying it
the coronation of Henry VIII
the beheading of Anne Boleyn
the day Powhatan gave Pocahontas
to white European men
Beethoven's first note pressed into a piano
Shakespeare's first play performed in The Globe Theatre
Custer's bad decision
the trail of tears
the blood soaked magenta fields of Gettysburg
the assassination at a bad play
of Abraham Lincoln
i shall remember Wounded Knee
the day suffragettes won their cause
the first words Anne Frank wrote in her secret diary
allied troops arriving

on the five beaches of Normandy
the first time John Fitzgerald Kennedy
laid eyes on Marilyn Monroe
and the day someone blew his brains
all over Jackie
the Washington Mall on the day
the people heard Dr. King say,
"I have a dream…"
the day Maya allowed her caged bird to sing
the moon landing and small steps on the surface
to spite Russia
the moment David Bowie decided
to make Ziggy into Stardust
the day Lou Reed released Wild Side
the moment the last of John Lennon
and Andy Warhol died
all told in an altoid tin

lover's leap

heading north
on the cocaine superhighway
coming out of jelico
there's a four story white cross
made from squared vinyl siding
nestled amidst pregnant mountains

a liquor store
a discount tobacco mart
and porntorium
two exits away
from stinking creek road

as you cross over
the Kentucky/Tennessee
state line into whitley county
there is a guard rail
signed
by couples
who've run off to elope
in the state
that gave the world
jack daniels whiskey
and a black velvet king
i stopped countin' when i saw
my mama's name the fourth time
she's where i get
all my southern optimism from

southern gothic

if there's one myth
a Baptist can dispel
it is the misconception
that all Christians are friendly

thin lipped women
become more so
when i enter a room

men succumb to a case
of the glancing can't help it's

it took a lot of suffering
books read
and introspection
to achieve this level of
fuck you
i don't give a shit

i love my life
i love living in my skin
i love my battle scars
i cherish my mistakes
as they became my teachers
i love my family in
all its grand dysfunction
we make spite look alluring

aw hell
let's go up

in the hay loft
talk about the power of forgiveness
and engage
in some heavy pettin'

the autism primer: year 18

this year will be a power struggle
with your child
as you attempt to balance
their need for independence
with their complete disconnect
from reality
and total lack of understanding with regards
to acceptable behaviors
responsibility
and consequences

you will spend much of this year
being screamed at
wishing you were dead
and envying empty nesters

explaining things like
showers must be taken daily
you can't wipe your shit on bath towels
or wipe cum on the floor

all whilst trying to instill
that being a person on the autism spectrum
doesn't give one a free pass
to be an abusive asshole to others
or one's environment

oh
let's not forget the guilt
you've carried around

from the day of your child's diagnosis

was it the vaccinations
something you should have eaten
or didn't eat while you were pregnant?
did you do this to them?

why were your children condemned?

yes
that reliable old friend will still be there
to keep you warm and reeling at night
a gnawing cancer in your gut
until the day
you end

stay positive
that's only
30 or 40 years away
friend

suicide tourism

besides being a great name
for a punk band
suicide tourism
is a growing trend
in switzerland
germans
brits
and americans
flocking to the monstrance
of neutrality
and lax euthanasia legislation
with a penchant for hiding
nazi-looted art
to eat chocolates laced
with sodium phenobarbital

"going to switzerland"
has become a euphemism
for offing oneself in the UK

(God, how I adore my saucy British cousins.)

Isn't it funny that in allegedly-civilized
free nations
their countrymen
don't even have the liberty
of choosing a dignified death?

★elected officials take note

when the power grid fails
we'll be coming
to eat you

soho diner

you know what
on second thought
drag me across the street
to the unisex bathroom
of a soho diner
and fuck me pinned
up against a nouveaux riche wall
your hands beneath my ass
the only necessary reality

street magician

the ruling class
wants you
embroiled

in the 24 hour news cycle

abortion debates
and racial tension

so you ignore
economic oppression

you've been duped
by a street magician

the information age
will be remembered

as the time humanity
was never more
misinformed

our neighbors would hate us

it was the moment
i felt the weight of you
that come hither look in your eyes
a crashing instant
when i contemplated
what we would be
we would make antony and cleopatra seem uncommitted
a passion so profound
it would negate my need for panties
i made the decision
not to want you
or the responsibility of your happiness
chose never to be the person
who complains you're never around
and when you're home don't lift a finger
i never want to be your freshest regret

what a perfect disaster we would be

our neighbors would hate us

we would go to home depot
and choose to paint the bathroom an almost puce shade of armageddon
we would watch fatal attraction together and immediately
    run to ikea
for more lamps and cutlery

scratching vinyl to a screeching stop

speakers and clothing flying
through rattling windows

we'd brawl over a bourbon bottle
some june night
and threaten to cut each other
with the jagged pieces
of a kenny rogers and the first edition album

perpetually polar
fucking or fighting
either way it would be noisy
we would drive the sidewalk to drink
all the pearls in the world
would fall from their strands
we would tire of crying
you would invalidate my every previous love poem

our car would eternally be waiting to plunge
from an icy bridge
in the deep south
midwinter
because i threatened to jump out and through the door open to
puke
and you swerved trying to grab for my
drunk ass
because we'd love each other more than we had collective sense
there must be a heaven for that

sepia toned lithograph

i find myself longing
to live inside
a sepia toned lithograph
from the civil war

you'd be shipped to the mysterious
far off north
while i embalmed bodies
along side Thomas Holmes
my apron covered with
the sins of man
on blood soaked battlefields of the south

after a thousand letters written
and lessons learned
you'd come back home to me
with half yourself blown off
so i would decide
as a good woman does
to love you
all the more

cement truck philosophy

a wise and loyal friend
who is a monk
once explained to me
the cement truck philosophy
to approaching life

"find a need, then fill it…"

and it never made more sense to me
than as i was sitting
dead still in traffic
on I-71 southbound this morning
for two hours

an eighty year old man
walked onto the expressway
and jumped out in front
of a giant green cement truck
with the enthusiasm
of a little brooklyn girl
playing double dutch

people are saying
it wasn't a suicide
he was addled
confused
suffering from dementia

to which i respond
all the more reason

dying in the united states dictates
you buck up and suffer through it
our views on euthanasia are archaic

no, folks

i believe
he was having what they call
a moment of clarity

and i'd like to think
right before the truck hit him
he smiled and closed his eyes

he had a need for peace
he filled it

posthumous letter*

hey louisville,
long time no hear from, don juan try hump fat
i'm about to get waynesburg on your stubborn ass
and i want you to know for years
i forgave you for blowing your head off,
hell,
i applauded your ballsy choice
you were nothing if not consistent
you were proof the most intelligent and keen amongst us
are prone to depression, suicide, and addiction,
because we understand how fucked up the world can be
and simply can't bear the soul sucking siege and insult of it
no one should be made to suffer,
but you should be alive now
we need your voice now
more than ever,
gonzo journalist,
who thought the best was behind you
and it had only just begun
n' don't you tell me all the best kentuckians die young and
grandly
you're dead as a damned door nail
you can't talk back
and aye, that's the rub, old friend
i'm so mad at you for going away

* full title 'posthumous letter mailed to the marvelous hunter s. thompson at his trashy extended stay suite nestled on the briny shores of hell's lake of fire'

if you weren't already dead
i'd shoot you again myself

love you, fucker
a

aruba

the poet in me says
lover man
to hell with this grind
the wasted time
why can't we
just run away
to aruba

pack a bag for every child
we're never going to have

buy two one-way plane tickets
hop on board with jive passports
newly assumed names
wearing oversized hats
me in garbo sunglasses
you wearing a camera about your neck
with no film inside
as there will be no return trip
to have the pictures developed

we'll sit on the beach
for the rest of our lives
with a ukulele that plays itself
an endless joint
and a bottomless margarita
its glass rim never shy of salt

i'll wear a yellow string bikini
not giving a damn about my scars

you can make dean martin eyes at me
all you like
sing off-key love songs
into campfire light

and when we die
on the same day
perfectly
hermit crabs
will drag us back into the sea

this day and for the rest of time

you know
it is true what *they* say

your entire life really does
flash before your eyes
the moment before a motor vehicle accident

my film reel cigarette burned
car crash footage
went precisely like this:

i saw my twin sons locked out of the house
in 18 degree weather
upon returning from school
to find their mother nowhere around & *unalive*
...this day and for the rest of time

i saw my mother's face
and thought how i wanted
to touch her downy warm cheek
one more time

i thought about my brother bob
and how i would not live to see him write
the great american novel

i saw the face of the man whom i am in love with

i thought about how happy i would be to see daddy
at the dinner table in heaven tonight

i saw my friends sarah, marissa, and sean
toasting to my existence

i thought about how grateful i am
to have been given this amazing life

thank you, god, whomever you are
alas
it is i who shall cover you
with a blanket of stars
this night

50 year plan

keep my mother proud of me

give my sons braggin' rights
love in their hearts
and wisdom in their minds

be the reason my father's sooty
fallen angel wings
spread wide
closer to the throne of god
when i do something right

perform a poem
at the inauguration
of the first female president

allow my deeds to accomodate
sleeping well at night

about the author

Alicia Young is a poet, editor, mother, former mortician, middling pianist, and above average tap dancer. She has the tongue of a harpy, the heart of a benevolent queen, the gall of a mad king, and is rumored to be a wee bit of a tramp. She is a modern day Southern belle, born on Kentucky's bourbon trail, and 7th great granddaughter of Pocahontas. She enjoys black coffee and Wild Turkey in the morning, complimented by a fine cigar at night. Her Electra complex is the stuff of legend. She makes a hobby of causing blonde, Republican women to cry. Her dog, Vinnie Pupparino, is a former mafioso turned pro-wrestler. Ms. Young is the baddest woman on the planet with a set of nunchaku while any southern rock is playing. She was previously published in The Long Islander, Cultural Weekly, American Funeral Director, The Vagina Gun, The Musophobist, The Montucky Review, Take-It-To-The-Streets-Poetry, The Juice Bar, The Moronic Ox Literary & Cultural Journal, and The Mas Tequila Review. Ms. Young is the author of *Hell on Heels*, poems by Alicia Young, released in 2012 by Lady-Lazarus Press.

www.ingramcontent.com/pod-product-compliance
Lightning Source LLC
LaVergne TN
LVHW041549070426
835507LV00011B/1007